PERSONAL DETAILS

NAME	
COMPANY NAME	
ADDRESS	
EMAIL	
PHONE NUMBER	
MOBILE NUMBER	

SHIFT HANDOVER

DATE		DAY	
NAME		RANK / GRADE	
TIME IN		TIME OUT	
DEPARTMENT		SUPERVISOR	
HANDOVER TIME			

HANDOVER DETAILS	
EQUIPMENT	
CONCERNS	

HANDOVER TO		STAFF NO.	
DATE IN		DATE OUT	
TIME IN		TIME OUT	

ACTIONS TO COMPLETE

NO.	ACTION	COMPLETED DATE
1		
2		
3		
4		
5		

COMPLETED ACTIONS

NO.	ACTION	COMPLETED DATE
1		
2		
3		
4		
5		

NOTES

_____
_____
_____
_____
_____
_____
_____

CLOSING SHIFT SIGNATURE	STARTING SHIFT SIGNATURE

SHIFT HANDOVER

DATE		DAY	
NAME		RANK / GRADE	
TIME IN		TIME OUT	
DEPARTMENT		SUPERVISOR	
HANDOVER TIME			

HANDOVER DETAILS	
EQUIPMENT	
CONCERNS	

HANDOVER TO		STAFF NO.	
DATE IN		DATE OUT	
TIME IN		TIME OUT	

ACTIONS TO COMPLETE

COMPLETED ACTIONS

NO.	ACTION	COMPLETED DATE
1		
2		
3		
4		
5		

NO.	ACTION	COMPLETED DATE
1		
2		
3		
4		
5		

NOTES

_____
_____
_____
_____
_____
_____
_____

CLOSING SHIFT SIGNATURE	STARTING SHIFT SIGNATURE

SHIFT HANDOVER

DATE		DAY	
NAME		RANK / GRADE	
TIME IN		TIME OUT	
DEPARTMENT		SUPERVISOR	
HANDOVER TIME			

HANDOVER DETAILS	
EQUIPMENT	
CONCERNS	

HANDOVER TO		STAFF NO.	
DATE IN		DATE OUT	
TIME IN		TIME OUT	

ACTIONS TO COMPLETE

NO.	ACTION	COMPLETED DATE
1		
2		
3		
4		
5		

COMPLETED ACTIONS

NO.	ACTION	COMPLETED DATE
1		
2		
3		
4		
5		

NOTES

_____

_____

_____

_____

_____

_____

_____

CLOSING SHIFT SIGNATURE	STARTING SHIFT SIGNATURE

SHIFT HANDOVER

DATE		DAY	
NAME		RANK / GRADE	
TIME IN		TIME OUT	
DEPARTMENT		SUPERVISOR	
HANDOVER TIME			

HANDOVER DETAILS	
EQUIPMENT	
CONCERNS	

HANDOVER TO		STAFF NO.	
DATE IN		DATE OUT	
TIME IN		TIME OUT	

ACTIONS TO COMPLETE

COMPLETED ACTIONS

NO.	ACTION	COMPLETED DATE
1		
2		
3		
4		
5		

NO.	ACTION	COMPLETED DATE
1		
2		
3		
4		
5		

NOTES

_____
_____
_____
_____
_____
_____
_____

CLOSING SHIFT SIGNATURE	STARTING SHIFT SIGNATURE

SHIFT HANDOVER

DATE		DAY	
NAME		RANK / GRADE	
TIME IN		TIME OUT	
DEPARTMENT		SUPERVISOR	
HANDOVER TIME			

HANDOVER DETAILS	
EQUIPMENT	
CONCERNS	

HANDOVER TO		STAFF NO.	
DATE IN		DATE OUT	
TIME IN		TIME OUT	

ACTIONS TO COMPLETE

NO.	ACTION	COMPLETED DATE
1		
2		
3		
4		
5		

COMPLETED ACTIONS

NO.	ACTION	COMPLETED DATE
1		
2		
3		
4		
5		

NOTES

CLOSING SHIFT SIGNATURE	STARTING SHIFT SIGNATURE

SHIFT HANDOVER

DATE		DAY	
NAME		RANK / GRADE	
TIME IN		TIME OUT	
DEPARTMENT		SUPERVISOR	
HANDOVER TIME			

HANDOVER DETAILS	
EQUIPMENT	
CONCERNS	

HANDOVER TO		STAFF NO.	
DATE IN		DATE OUT	
TIME IN		TIME OUT	

ACTIONS TO COMPLETE

NO.	ACTION	COMPLETED DATE
1		
2		
3		
4		
5		

COMPLETED ACTIONS

NO.	ACTION	COMPLETED DATE
1		
2		
3		
4		
5		

NOTES

_____
_____
_____
_____
_____
_____
_____
_____

CLOSING SHIFT SIGNATURE	STARTING SHIFT SIGNATURE

SHIFT HANDOVER

DATE		DAY	
NAME		RANK / GRADE	
TIME IN		TIME OUT	
DEPARTMENT		SUPERVISOR	
HANDOVER TIME			

HANDOVER DETAILS	
EQUIPMENT	
CONCERNS	

HANDOVER TO		STAFF NO.	
DATE IN		DATE OUT	
TIME IN		TIME OUT	

ACTIONS TO COMPLETE

NO.	ACTION	COMPLETED DATE
1		
2		
3		
4		
5		

COMPLETED ACTIONS

NO.	ACTION	COMPLETED DATE
1		
2		
3		
4		
5		

NOTES

_____
_____
_____
_____
_____
_____
_____
_____

CLOSING SHIFT SIGNATURE	STARTING SHIFT SIGNATURE

SHIFT HANDOVER

DATE		DAY	
NAME		RANK / GRADE	
TIME IN		TIME OUT	
DEPARTMENT		SUPERVISOR	
HANDOVER TIME			

HANDOVER DETAILS	
EQUIPMENT	
CONCERNS	

HANDOVER TO		STAFF NO.	
DATE IN		DATE OUT	
TIME IN		TIME OUT	

ACTIONS TO COMPLETE

NO.	ACTION	COMPLETED DATE
1		
2		
3		
4		
5		

COMPLETED ACTIONS

NO.	ACTION	COMPLETED DATE
1		
2		
3		
4		
5		

NOTES

_____
_____
_____
_____
_____
_____
_____
_____

CLOSING SHIFT SIGNATURE	STARTING SHIFT SIGNATURE

SHIFT HANDOVER

DATE		DAY	
NAME		RANK / GRADE	
TIME IN		TIME OUT	
DEPARTMENT		SUPERVISOR	
HANDOVER TIME			

HANDOVER DETAILS	

EQUIPMENT	

CONCERNS	

HANDOVER TO		STAFF NO.	
DATE IN		DATE OUT	
TIME IN		TIME OUT	

ACTIONS TO COMPLETE

NO.	ACTION	COMPLETED DATE
1		
2		
3		
4		
5		

COMPLETED ACTIONS

NO.	ACTION	COMPLETED DATE
1		
2		
3		
4		
5		

NOTES

_____

_____

_____

_____

_____

_____

_____

_____

CLOSING SHIFT SIGNATURE	STARTING SHIFT SIGNATURE

SHIFT HANDOVER

DATE		DAY	
NAME		RANK / GRADE	
TIME IN		TIME OUT	
DEPARTMENT		SUPERVISOR	
HANDOVER TIME			

HANDOVER DETAILS	
EQUIPMENT	
CONCERNS	

HANDOVER TO		STAFF NO.	
DATE IN		DATE OUT	
TIME IN		TIME OUT	

ACTIONS TO COMPLETE

COMPLETED ACTIONS

NO.	ACTION	COMPLETED DATE
1		
2		
3		
4		
5		

NO.	ACTION	COMPLETED DATE
1		
2		
3		
4		
5		

NOTES

_____
_____
_____
_____
_____
_____
_____
_____
_____

CLOSING SHIFT SIGNATURE	STARTING SHIFT SIGNATURE

SHIFT HANDOVER

DATE		DAY	
NAME		RANK / GRADE	
TIME IN		TIME OUT	
DEPARTMENT		SUPERVISOR	
HANDOVER TIME			

HANDOVER DETAILS	
EQUIPMENT	
CONCERNS	

HANDOVER TO		STAFF NO.	
DATE IN		DATE OUT	
TIME IN		TIME OUT	

ACTIONS TO COMPLETE

NO.	ACTION	COMPLETED DATE
1		
2		
3		
4		
5		

COMPLETED ACTIONS

NO.	ACTION	COMPLETED DATE
1		
2		
3		
4		
5		

NOTES

_____
_____
_____
_____
_____
_____
_____

CLOSING SHIFT SIGNATURE	STARTING SHIFT SIGNATURE

SHIFT HANDOVER

DATE		DAY	
NAME		RANK / GRADE	
TIME IN		TIME OUT	
DEPARTMENT		SUPERVISOR	
HANDOVER TIME			

HANDOVER DETAILS	

EQUIPMENT	

CONCERNS	

HANDOVER TO		STAFF NO.	
DATE IN		DATE OUT	
TIME IN		TIME OUT	

ACTIONS TO COMPLETE

NO.	ACTION	COMPLETED DATE
1		
2		
3		
4		
5		

COMPLETED ACTIONS

NO.	ACTION	COMPLETED DATE
1		
2		
3		
4		
5		

NOTES

_____
_____
_____
_____
_____
_____
_____
_____

CLOSING SHIFT SIGNATURE	STARTING SHIFT SIGNATURE

SHIFT HANDOVER

DATE		DAY	
NAME		RANK / GRADE	
TIME IN		TIME OUT	
DEPARTMENT		SUPERVISOR	
HANDOVER TIME			

HANDOVER DETAILS	
EQUIPMENT	
CONCERNS	

HANDOVER TO		STAFF NO.	
DATE IN		DATE OUT	
TIME IN		TIME OUT	

ACTIONS TO COMPLETE

NO.	ACTION	COMPLETED DATE
1		
2		
3		
4		
5		

COMPLETED ACTIONS

NO.	ACTION	COMPLETED DATE
1		
2		
3		
4		
5		

NOTES

_____
_____
_____
_____
_____
_____
_____
_____

CLOSING SHIFT SIGNATURE	STARTING SHIFT SIGNATURE

SHIFT HANDOVER

DATE		DAY	
NAME		RANK / GRADE	
TIME IN		TIME OUT	
DEPARTMENT		SUPERVISOR	
HANDOVER TIME			

HANDOVER DETAILS	
EQUIPMENT	
CONCERNS	

HANDOVER TO		STAFF NO.	
DATE IN		DATE OUT	
TIME IN		TIME OUT	

ACTIONS TO COMPLETE

NO.	ACTION	COMPLETED DATE
1		
2		
3		
4		
5		

COMPLETED ACTIONS

NO.	ACTION	COMPLETED DATE
1		
2		
3		
4		
5		

NOTES

_____

_____

_____

_____

_____

_____

_____

CLOSING SHIFT SIGNATURE	STARTING SHIFT SIGNATURE

SHIFT HANDOVER

DATE		DAY	
NAME		RANK / GRADE	
TIME IN		TIME OUT	
DEPARTMENT		SUPERVISOR	
HANDOVER TIME			

HANDOVER DETAILS	
EQUIPMENT	
CONCERNS	

HANDOVER TO		STAFF NO.	
DATE IN		DATE OUT	
TIME IN		TIME OUT	

ACTIONS TO COMPLETE

NO.	ACTION	COMPLETED DATE
1		
2		
3		
4		
5		

COMPLETED ACTIONS

NO.	ACTION	COMPLETED DATE
1		
2		
3		
4		
5		

NOTES

_____

_____

_____

_____

_____

_____

_____

_____

CLOSING SHIFT SIGNATURE	STARTING SHIFT SIGNATURE

SHIFT HANDOVER

DATE		DAY	
NAME		RANK / GRADE	
TIME IN		TIME OUT	
DEPARTMENT		SUPERVISOR	
HANDOVER TIME			

HANDOVER DETAILS	
EQUIPMENT	
CONCERNS	

HANDOVER TO		STAFF NO.	
DATE IN		DATE OUT	
TIME IN		TIME OUT	

ACTIONS TO COMPLETE

COMPLETED ACTIONS

NO.	ACTION	COMPLETED DATE
1		
2		
3		
4		
5		

NO.	ACTION	COMPLETED DATE
1		
2		
3		
4		
5		

NOTES

_____

_____

_____

_____

_____

_____

_____

_____

CLOSING SHIFT SIGNATURE | **STARTING SHIFT SIGNATURE**

SHIFT HANDOVER

DATE		DAY	
NAME		RANK / GRADE	
TIME IN		TIME OUT	
DEPARTMENT		SUPERVISOR	
HANDOVER TIME			

HANDOVER DETAILS	
EQUIPMENT	
CONCERNS	

HANDOVER TO		STAFF NO.	
DATE IN		DATE OUT	
TIME IN		TIME OUT	

ACTIONS TO COMPLETE

NO.	ACTION	COMPLETED DATE
1		
2		
3		
4		
5		

COMPLETED ACTIONS

NO.	ACTION	COMPLETED DATE
1		
2		
3		
4		
5		

NOTES

_____
_____
_____
_____
_____
_____
_____
_____

CLOSING SHIFT SIGNATURE	STARTING SHIFT SIGNATURE

SHIFT HANDOVER

DATE		DAY	
NAME		RANK / GRADE	
TIME IN		TIME OUT	
DEPARTMENT		SUPERVISOR	
HANDOVER TIME			

HANDOVER DETAILS	
EQUIPMENT	
CONCERNS	

HANDOVER TO		STAFF NO.	
DATE IN		DATE OUT	
TIME IN		TIME OUT	

ACTIONS TO COMPLETE

NO.	ACTION	COMPLETED DATE
1		
2		
3		
4		
5		

COMPLETED ACTIONS

NO.	ACTION	COMPLETED DATE
1		
2		
3		
4		
5		

NOTES

_____
_____
_____
_____
_____
_____
_____
_____

CLOSING SHIFT SIGNATURE	STARTING SHIFT SIGNATURE

SHIFT HANDOVER

DATE		DAY	
NAME		RANK / GRADE	
TIME IN		TIME OUT	
DEPARTMENT		SUPERVISOR	
HANDOVER TIME			

HANDOVER DETAILS	
EQUIPMENT	
CONCERNS	

HANDOVER TO		STAFF NO.	
DATE IN		DATE OUT	
TIME IN		TIME OUT	

ACTIONS TO COMPLETE

NO.	ACTION	COMPLETED DATE
1		
2		
3		
4		
5		

COMPLETED ACTIONS

NO.	ACTION	COMPLETED DATE
1		
2		
3		
4		
5		

NOTES

_____
_____
_____
_____
_____
_____
_____

CLOSING SHIFT SIGNATURE	STARTING SHIFT SIGNATURE

SHIFT HANDOVER

DATE		DAY	
NAME		RANK / GRADE	
TIME IN		TIME OUT	
DEPARTMENT		SUPERVISOR	
HANDOVER TIME			

HANDOVER DETAILS	
EQUIPMENT	
CONCERNS	

HANDOVER TO		STAFF NO.	
DATE IN		DATE OUT	
TIME IN		TIME OUT	

ACTIONS TO COMPLETE

COMPLETED ACTIONS

NO.	ACTION	COMPLETED DATE	NO.	ACTION	COMPLETED DATE
1			1		
2			2		
3			3		
4			4		
5			5		

NOTES

_____
_____
_____
_____
_____
_____
_____
_____

CLOSING SHIFT SIGNATURE	STARTING SHIFT SIGNATURE

SHIFT HANDOVER

DATE		DAY	
NAME		RANK / GRADE	
TIME IN		TIME OUT	
DEPARTMENT		SUPERVISOR	
HANDOVER TIME			

HANDOVER DETAILS	
EQUIPMENT	
CONCERNS	

HANDOVER TO		STAFF NO.	
DATE IN		DATE OUT	
TIME IN		TIME OUT	

ACTIONS TO COMPLETE

NO.	ACTION	COMPLETED DATE
1		
2		
3		
4		
5		

COMPLETED ACTIONS

NO.	ACTION	COMPLETED DATE
1		
2		
3		
4		
5		

NOTES

_____
_____
_____
_____
_____
_____
_____
_____

CLOSING SHIFT SIGNATURE	STARTING SHIFT SIGNATURE

SHIFT HANDOVER

DATE		DAY	
NAME		RANK / GRADE	
TIME IN		TIME OUT	
DEPARTMENT		SUPERVISOR	
HANDOVER TIME			

HANDOVER DETAILS	
EQUIPMENT	
CONCERNS	

HANDOVER TO		STAFF NO.	
DATE IN		DATE OUT	
TIME IN		TIME OUT	

ACTIONS TO COMPLETE   COMPLETED ACTIONS

NO.	ACTION	COMPLETED DATE		NO.	ACTION	COMPLETED DATE
1				1		
2				2		
3				3		
4				4		
5				5		

NOTES

_____
_____
_____
_____
_____
_____
_____
_____

CLOSING SHIFT SIGNATURE	STARTING SHIFT SIGNATURE

SHIFT HANDOVER

DATE		DAY	
NAME		RANK / GRADE	
TIME IN		TIME OUT	
DEPARTMENT		SUPERVISOR	
HANDOVER TIME			

HANDOVER DETAILS	
EQUIPMENT	
CONCERNS	

HANDOVER TO		STAFF NO.	
DATE IN		DATE OUT	
TIME IN		TIME OUT	

ACTIONS TO COMPLETE

NO.	ACTION	COMPLETED DATE
1		
2		
3		
4		
5		

COMPLETED ACTIONS

NO.	ACTION	COMPLETED DATE
1		
2		
3		
4		
5		

NOTES

_____

_____

_____

_____

_____

_____

_____

_____

CLOSING SHIFT SIGNATURE	STARTING SHIFT SIGNATURE

SHIFT HANDOVER

DATE		DAY	
NAME		RANK / GRADE	
TIME IN		TIME OUT	
DEPARTMENT		SUPERVISOR	
HANDOVER TIME			

HANDOVER DETAILS	
EQUIPMENT	
CONCERNS	

HANDOVER TO		STAFF NO.	
DATE IN		DATE OUT	
TIME IN		TIME OUT	

ACTIONS TO COMPLETE

COMPLETED ACTIONS

NO.	ACTION	COMPLETED DATE
1		
2		
3		
4		
5		

NO.	ACTION	COMPLETED DATE
1		
2		
3		
4		
5		

NOTES

_____

_____

_____

_____

_____

_____

_____

_____

CLOSING SHIFT SIGNATURE	STARTING SHIFT SIGNATURE

SHIFT HANDOVER

DATE		DAY	
NAME		RANK / GRADE	
TIME IN		TIME OUT	
DEPARTMENT		SUPERVISOR	
HANDOVER TIME			

HANDOVER DETAILS	
EQUIPMENT	
CONCERNS	

HANDOVER TO		STAFF NO.	
DATE IN		DATE OUT	
TIME IN		TIME OUT	

ACTIONS TO COMPLETE   COMPLETED ACTIONS

NO.	ACTION	COMPLETED DATE	NO.	ACTION	COMPLETED DATE
1			1		
2			2		
3			3		
4			4		
5			5		

NOTES

_____
_____
_____
_____
_____
_____
_____
_____

CLOSING SHIFT SIGNATURE	STARTING SHIFT SIGNATURE

SHIFT HANDOVER

DATE		DAY	
NAME		RANK / GRADE	
TIME IN		TIME OUT	
DEPARTMENT		SUPERVISOR	
HANDOVER TIME			

HANDOVER DETAILS	
EQUIPMENT	
CONCERNS	

HANDOVER TO		STAFF NO.	
DATE IN		DATE OUT	
TIME IN		TIME OUT	

ACTIONS TO COMPLETE

COMPLETED ACTIONS

NO.	ACTION	COMPLETED DATE
1		
2		
3		
4		
5		

NO.	ACTION	COMPLETED DATE
1		
2		
3		
4		
5		

NOTES

_____
_____
_____
_____
_____
_____
_____
_____

CLOSING SHIFT SIGNATURE	STARTING SHIFT SIGNATURE

SHIFT HANDOVER

DATE		DAY	
NAME		RANK / GRADE	
TIME IN		TIME OUT	
DEPARTMENT		SUPERVISOR	
HANDOVER TIME			

HANDOVER DETAILS	

EQUIPMENT	

CONCERNS	

HANDOVER TO		STAFF NO.	
DATE IN		DATE OUT	
TIME IN		TIME OUT	

ACTIONS TO COMPLETE

COMPLETED ACTIONS

NO.	ACTION	COMPLETED DATE
1		
2		
3		
4		
5		

NO.	ACTION	COMPLETED DATE
1		
2		
3		
4		
5		

NOTES

_____
_____
_____
_____
_____
_____
_____
_____

CLOSING SHIFT SIGNATURE	STARTING SHIFT SIGNATURE

SHIFT HANDOVER

DATE		DAY	
NAME		RANK / GRADE	
TIME IN		TIME OUT	
DEPARTMENT		SUPERVISOR	
HANDOVER TIME			

HANDOVER DETAILS	
EQUIPMENT	
CONCERNS	

HANDOVER TO		STAFF NO.	
DATE IN		DATE OUT	
TIME IN		TIME OUT	

ACTIONS TO COMPLETE

NO.	ACTION	COMPLETED DATE
1		
2		
3		
4		
5		

COMPLETED ACTIONS

NO.	ACTION	COMPLETED DATE
1		
2		
3		
4		
5		

NOTES

_____
_____
_____
_____
_____
_____
_____
_____

CLOSING SHIFT SIGNATURE	STARTING SHIFT SIGNATURE

SHIFT HANDOVER

DATE		DAY	
NAME		RANK / GRADE	
TIME IN		TIME OUT	
DEPARTMENT		SUPERVISOR	
HANDOVER TIME			

HANDOVER DETAILS	

EQUIPMENT	

CONCERNS	

HANDOVER TO		STAFF NO.	
DATE IN		DATE OUT	
TIME IN		TIME OUT	

ACTIONS TO COMPLETE

NO.	ACTION	COMPLETED DATE
1		
2		
3		
4		
5		

COMPLETED ACTIONS

NO.	ACTION	COMPLETED DATE
1		
2		
3		
4		
5		

NOTES

_____

_____

_____

_____

_____

_____

_____

_____

CLOSING SHIFT SIGNATURE	STARTING SHIFT SIGNATURE

SHIFT HANDOVER

DATE		DAY	
NAME		RANK / GRADE	
TIME IN		TIME OUT	
DEPARTMENT		SUPERVISOR	
HANDOVER TIME			

HANDOVER DETAILS	

EQUIPMENT	

CONCERNS	

HANDOVER TO		STAFF NO.	
DATE IN		DATE OUT	
TIME IN		TIME OUT	

ACTIONS TO COMPLETE

NO.	ACTION	COMPLETED DATE
1		
2		
3		
4		
5		

COMPLETED ACTIONS

NO.	ACTION	COMPLETED DATE
1		
2		
3		
4		
5		

NOTES

_____

_____

_____

_____

_____

_____

_____

_____

CLOSING SHIFT SIGNATURE	STARTING SHIFT SIGNATURE

SHIFT HANDOVER

DATE		DAY	
NAME		RANK / GRADE	
TIME IN		TIME OUT	
DEPARTMENT		SUPERVISOR	
HANDOVER TIME			

HANDOVER DETAILS	
EQUIPMENT	
CONCERNS	

HANDOVER TO		STAFF NO.	
DATE IN		DATE OUT	
TIME IN		TIME OUT	

ACTIONS TO COMPLETE

NO.	ACTION	COMPLETED DATE
1		
2		
3		
4		
5		

COMPLETED ACTIONS

NO.	ACTION	COMPLETED DATE
1		
2		
3		
4		
5		

NOTES

_____
_____
_____
_____
_____
_____
_____
_____

CLOSING SHIFT SIGNATURE	STARTING SHIFT SIGNATURE

SHIFT HANDOVER

DATE		DAY	
NAME		RANK / GRADE	
TIME IN		TIME OUT	
DEPARTMENT		SUPERVISOR	
HANDOVER TIME			

HANDOVER DETAILS	
EQUIPMENT	
CONCERNS	

HANDOVER TO		STAFF NO.	
DATE IN		DATE OUT	
TIME IN		TIME OUT	

ACTIONS TO COMPLETE   COMPLETED ACTIONS

NO.	ACTION	COMPLETED DATE	NO.	ACTION	COMPLETED DATE
1			1		
2			2		
3			3		
4			4		
5			5		

NOTES

_____

_____

_____

_____

_____

_____

_____

_____

CLOSING SHIFT SIGNATURE	**STARTING SHIFT SIGNATURE**

SHIFT HANDOVER

DATE		DAY	
NAME		RANK / GRADE	
TIME IN		TIME OUT	
DEPARTMENT		SUPERVISOR	
HANDOVER TIME			

HANDOVER DETAILS	
EQUIPMENT	
CONCERNS	

HANDOVER TO		STAFF NO.	
DATE IN		DATE OUT	
TIME IN		TIME OUT	

ACTIONS TO COMPLETE   COMPLETED ACTIONS

NO.	ACTION	COMPLETED DATE	NO.	ACTION	COMPLETED DATE
1			1		
2			2		
3			3		
4			4		
5			5		

NOTES

_____
_____
_____
_____
_____
_____
_____
_____

CLOSING SHIFT SIGNATURE	STARTING SHIFT SIGNATURE

SHIFT HANDOVER

DATE		DAY	
NAME		RANK / GRADE	
TIME IN		TIME OUT	
DEPARTMENT		SUPERVISOR	
HANDOVER TIME			

HANDOVER DETAILS	
EQUIPMENT	
CONCERNS	

HANDOVER TO		STAFF NO.	
DATE IN		DATE OUT	
TIME IN		TIME OUT	

ACTIONS TO COMPLETE

NO.	ACTION	COMPLETED DATE
1		
2		
3		
4		
5		

COMPLETED ACTIONS

NO.	ACTION	COMPLETED DATE
1		
2		
3		
4		
5		

NOTES

_____
_____
_____
_____
_____
_____
_____
_____

CLOSING SHIFT SIGNATURE	STARTING SHIFT SIGNATURE

SHIFT HANDOVER

DATE		DAY	
NAME		RANK / GRADE	
TIME IN		TIME OUT	
DEPARTMENT		SUPERVISOR	
HANDOVER TIME			

HANDOVER DETAILS	
EQUIPMENT	
CONCERNS	

HANDOVER TO		STAFF NO.	
DATE IN		DATE OUT	
TIME IN		TIME OUT	

ACTIONS TO COMPLETE

NO.	ACTION	COMPLETED DATE
1		
2		
3		
4		
5		

COMPLETED ACTIONS

NO.	ACTION	COMPLETED DATE
1		
2		
3		
4		
5		

NOTES

_____
_____
_____
_____
_____
_____
_____
_____

CLOSING SHIFT SIGNATURE	STARTING SHIFT SIGNATURE

SHIFT HANDOVER

DATE		DAY	
NAME		RANK / GRADE	
TIME IN		TIME OUT	
DEPARTMENT		SUPERVISOR	
HANDOVER TIME			

HANDOVER DETAILS	
EQUIPMENT	
CONCERNS	

HANDOVER TO		STAFF NO.	
DATE IN		DATE OUT	
TIME IN		TIME OUT	

ACTIONS TO COMPLETE

NO.	ACTION	COMPLETED DATE
1		
2		
3		
4		
5		

COMPLETED ACTIONS

NO.	ACTION	COMPLETED DATE
1		
2		
3		
4		
5		

NOTES

_____

_____

_____

_____

_____

_____

_____

_____

CLOSING SHIFT SIGNATURE	STARTING SHIFT SIGNATURE

SHIFT HANDOVER

DATE		DAY	
NAME		RANK / GRADE	
TIME IN		TIME OUT	
DEPARTMENT		SUPERVISOR	
HANDOVER TIME			

HANDOVER DETAILS	
EQUIPMENT	
CONCERNS	

HANDOVER TO		STAFF NO.	
DATE IN		DATE OUT	
TIME IN		TIME OUT	

ACTIONS TO COMPLETE   COMPLETED ACTIONS

NO.	ACTION	COMPLETED DATE	NO.	ACTION	COMPLETED DATE
1			1		
2			2		
3			3		
4			4		
5			5		

NOTES

_____
_____
_____
_____
_____
_____
_____
_____

CLOSING SHIFT SIGNATURE	STARTING SHIFT SIGNATURE

SHIFT HANDOVER

DATE		DAY	
NAME		RANK / GRADE	
TIME IN		TIME OUT	
DEPARTMENT		SUPERVISOR	
HANDOVER TIME			

HANDOVER DETAILS	
EQUIPMENT	
CONCERNS	

HANDOVER TO		STAFF NO.	
DATE IN		DATE OUT	
TIME IN		TIME OUT	

ACTIONS TO COMPLETE

NO.	ACTION	COMPLETED DATE
1		
2		
3		
4		
5		

COMPLETED ACTIONS

NO.	ACTION	COMPLETED DATE
1		
2		
3		
4		
5		

NOTES

_____

_____

_____

_____

_____

_____

_____

_____

CLOSING SHIFT SIGNATURE	STARTING SHIFT SIGNATURE

SHIFT HANDOVER

DATE		DAY	
NAME		RANK / GRADE	
TIME IN		TIME OUT	
DEPARTMENT		SUPERVISOR	
HANDOVER TIME			

HANDOVER DETAILS	
EQUIPMENT	
CONCERNS	

HANDOVER TO		STAFF NO.	
DATE IN		DATE OUT	
TIME IN		TIME OUT	

ACTIONS TO COMPLETE

NO.	ACTION	COMPLETED DATE
1		
2		
3		
4		
5		

COMPLETED ACTIONS

NO.	ACTION	COMPLETED DATE
1		
2		
3		
4		
5		

NOTES

_____

_____

_____

_____

_____

_____

_____

_____

CLOSING SHIFT SIGNATURE	STARTING SHIFT SIGNATURE

SHIFT HANDOVER

DATE		DAY	
NAME		RANK / GRADE	
TIME IN		TIME OUT	
DEPARTMENT		SUPERVISOR	
HANDOVER TIME			

HANDOVER DETAILS	
EQUIPMENT	
CONCERNS	

HANDOVER TO		STAFF NO.	
DATE IN		DATE OUT	
TIME IN		TIME OUT	

ACTIONS TO COMPLETE

COMPLETED ACTIONS

NO.	ACTION	COMPLETED DATE
1		
2		
3		
4		
5		

NO.	ACTION	COMPLETED DATE
1		
2		
3		
4		
5		

NOTES

_____

_____

_____

_____

_____

_____

_____

_____

CLOSING SHIFT SIGNATURE	STARTING SHIFT SIGNATURE

SHIFT HANDOVER

DATE		DAY	
NAME		RANK / GRADE	
TIME IN		TIME OUT	
DEPARTMENT		SUPERVISOR	
HANDOVER TIME			

HANDOVER DETAILS	
EQUIPMENT	
CONCERNS	

HANDOVER TO		STAFF NO.	
DATE IN		DATE OUT	
TIME IN		TIME OUT	

ACTIONS TO COMPLETE

COMPLETED ACTIONS

NO.	ACTION	COMPLETED DATE	NO.	ACTION	COMPLETED DATE
1			1		
2			2		
3			3		
4			4		
5			5		

NOTES

_____
_____
_____
_____
_____
_____
_____
_____

CLOSING SHIFT SIGNATURE	STARTING SHIFT SIGNATURE

SHIFT HANDOVER

DATE		DAY	
NAME		RANK / GRADE	
TIME IN		TIME OUT	
DEPARTMENT		SUPERVISOR	
HANDOVER TIME			

HANDOVER DETAILS	
EQUIPMENT	
CONCERNS	

HANDOVER TO		STAFF NO.	
DATE IN		DATE OUT	
TIME IN		TIME OUT	

ACTIONS TO COMPLETE

NO.	ACTION	COMPLETED DATE
1		
2		
3		
4		
5		

COMPLETED ACTIONS

NO.	ACTION	COMPLETED DATE
1		
2		
3		
4		
5		

NOTES

_____

_____

_____

_____

_____

_____

_____

CLOSING SHIFT SIGNATURE	STARTING SHIFT SIGNATURE

SHIFT HANDOVER

DATE		DAY	
NAME		RANK / GRADE	
TIME IN		TIME OUT	
DEPARTMENT		SUPERVISOR	
HANDOVER TIME			

HANDOVER DETAILS	
EQUIPMENT	
CONCERNS	

HANDOVER TO		STAFF NO.	
DATE IN		DATE OUT	
TIME IN		TIME OUT	

ACTIONS TO COMPLETE

NO.	ACTION	COMPLETED DATE
1		
2		
3		
4		
5		

COMPLETED ACTIONS

NO.	ACTION	COMPLETED DATE
1		
2		
3		
4		
5		

NOTES

_____
_____
_____
_____
_____
_____
_____
_____

CLOSING SHIFT SIGNATURE	STARTING SHIFT SIGNATURE

SHIFT HANDOVER

DATE		DAY	
NAME		RANK / GRADE	
TIME IN		TIME OUT	
DEPARTMENT		SUPERVISOR	
HANDOVER TIME			

HANDOVER DETAILS	
EQUIPMENT	
CONCERNS	

HANDOVER TO		STAFF NO.	
DATE IN		DATE OUT	
TIME IN		TIME OUT	

ACTIONS TO COMPLETE

NO.	ACTION	COMPLETED DATE
1		
2		
3		
4		
5		

COMPLETED ACTIONS

NO.	ACTION	COMPLETED DATE
1		
2		
3		
4		
5		

NOTES

_____
_____
_____
_____
_____
_____
_____
_____

CLOSING SHIFT SIGNATURE	STARTING SHIFT SIGNATURE

SHIFT HANDOVER

DATE		DAY	
NAME		RANK / GRADE	
TIME IN		TIME OUT	
DEPARTMENT		SUPERVISOR	
HANDOVER TIME			

HANDOVER DETAILS	

EQUIPMENT	

CONCERNS	

HANDOVER TO		STAFF NO.	
DATE IN		DATE OUT	
TIME IN		TIME OUT	

ACTIONS TO COMPLETE

NO.	ACTION	COMPLETED DATE
1		
2		
3		
4		
5		

COMPLETED ACTIONS

NO.	ACTION	COMPLETED DATE
1		
2		
3		
4		
5		

NOTES

_____
_____
_____
_____
_____
_____
_____
_____

CLOSING SHIFT SIGNATURE	STARTING SHIFT SIGNATURE

SHIFT HANDOVER

DATE		DAY	
NAME		RANK / GRADE	
TIME IN		TIME OUT	
DEPARTMENT		SUPERVISOR	
HANDOVER TIME			

HANDOVER DETAILS	
EQUIPMENT	
CONCERNS	

HANDOVER TO		STAFF NO.	
DATE IN		DATE OUT	
TIME IN		TIME OUT	

ACTIONS TO COMPLETE

COMPLETED ACTIONS

NO.	ACTION	COMPLETED DATE
1		
2		
3		
4		
5		

NO.	ACTION	COMPLETED DATE
1		
2		
3		
4		
5		

NOTES

_____

_____

_____

_____

_____

_____

_____

_____

CLOSING SHIFT SIGNATURE	STARTING SHIFT SIGNATURE

SHIFT HANDOVER

DATE		DAY	
NAME		RANK / GRADE	
TIME IN		TIME OUT	
DEPARTMENT		SUPERVISOR	
HANDOVER TIME			

HANDOVER DETAILS	
EQUIPMENT	
CONCERNS	

HANDOVER TO		STAFF NO.	
DATE IN		DATE OUT	
TIME IN		TIME OUT	

ACTIONS TO COMPLETE   COMPLETED ACTIONS

NO.	ACTION	COMPLETED DATE	NO.	ACTION	COMPLETED DATE
1			1		
2			2		
3			3		
4			4		
5			5		

NOTES

_____
_____
_____
_____
_____
_____
_____
_____

CLOSING SHIFT SIGNATURE	STARTING SHIFT SIGNATURE

SHIFT HANDOVER

DATE		DAY	
NAME		RANK / GRADE	
TIME IN		TIME OUT	
DEPARTMENT		SUPERVISOR	
HANDOVER TIME			

HANDOVER DETAILS	
EQUIPMENT	
CONCERNS	

HANDOVER TO		STAFF NO.	
DATE IN		DATE OUT	
TIME IN		TIME OUT	

ACTIONS TO COMPLETE

COMPLETED ACTIONS

NO.	ACTION	COMPLETED DATE
1		
2		
3		
4		
5		

NO.	ACTION	COMPLETED DATE
1		
2		
3		
4		
5		

NOTES

_____
_____
_____
_____
_____
_____
_____
_____

CLOSING SHIFT SIGNATURE	STARTING SHIFT SIGNATURE

SHIFT HANDOVER

DATE		DAY	
NAME		RANK / GRADE	
TIME IN		TIME OUT	
DEPARTMENT		SUPERVISOR	
HANDOVER TIME			

HANDOVER DETAILS	
EQUIPMENT	
CONCERNS	

HANDOVER TO		STAFF NO.	
DATE IN		DATE OUT	
TIME IN		TIME OUT	

ACTIONS TO COMPLETE

NO.	ACTION	COMPLETED DATE
1		
2		
3		
4		
5		

COMPLETED ACTIONS

NO.	ACTION	COMPLETED DATE
1		
2		
3		
4		
5		

NOTES

CLOSING SHIFT SIGNATURE	STARTING SHIFT SIGNATURE

SHIFT HANDOVER

DATE		DAY	
NAME		RANK / GRADE	
TIME IN		TIME OUT	
DEPARTMENT		SUPERVISOR	
HANDOVER TIME			

HANDOVER DETAILS	
EQUIPMENT	
CONCERNS	

HANDOVER TO		STAFF NO.	
DATE IN		DATE OUT	
TIME IN		TIME OUT	

ACTIONS TO COMPLETE

NO.	ACTION	COMPLETED DATE
1		
2		
3		
4		
5		

COMPLETED ACTIONS

NO.	ACTION	COMPLETED DATE
1		
2		
3		
4		
5		

NOTES

_____
_____
_____
_____
_____
_____
_____

CLOSING SHIFT SIGNATURE	STARTING SHIFT SIGNATURE

SHIFT HANDOVER

DATE		DAY	
NAME		RANK / GRADE	
TIME IN		TIME OUT	
DEPARTMENT		SUPERVISOR	
HANDOVER TIME			

HANDOVER DETAILS	
EQUIPMENT	
CONCERNS	

HANDOVER TO		STAFF NO.	
DATE IN		DATE OUT	
TIME IN		TIME OUT	

ACTIONS TO COMPLETE

NO.	ACTION	COMPLETED DATE
1		
2		
3		
4		
5		

COMPLETED ACTIONS

NO.	ACTION	COMPLETED DATE
1		
2		
3		
4		
5		

NOTES

_____
_____
_____
_____
_____
_____
_____
_____

CLOSING SHIFT SIGNATURE	STARTING SHIFT SIGNATURE

SHIFT HANDOVER

DATE		DAY	
NAME		RANK / GRADE	
TIME IN		TIME OUT	
DEPARTMENT		SUPERVISOR	
HANDOVER TIME			

HANDOVER DETAILS	
EQUIPMENT	
CONCERNS	

HANDOVER TO		STAFF NO.	
DATE IN		DATE OUT	
TIME IN		TIME OUT	

ACTIONS TO COMPLETE

NO.	ACTION	COMPLETED DATE
1		
2		
3		
4		
5		

COMPLETED ACTIONS

NO.	ACTION	COMPLETED DATE
1		
2		
3		
4		
5		

NOTES

_____

_____

_____

_____

_____

_____

_____

CLOSING SHIFT SIGNATURE	STARTING SHIFT SIGNATURE

SHIFT HANDOVER

DATE		DAY	
NAME		RANK / GRADE	
TIME IN		TIME OUT	
DEPARTMENT		SUPERVISOR	
HANDOVER TIME			

HANDOVER DETAILS	
EQUIPMENT	
CONCERNS	

HANDOVER TO		STAFF NO.	
DATE IN		DATE OUT	
TIME IN		TIME OUT	

ACTIONS TO COMPLETE

NO.	ACTION	COMPLETED DATE
1		
2		
3		
4		
5		

COMPLETED ACTIONS

NO.	ACTION	COMPLETED DATE
1		
2		
3		
4		
5		

NOTES

_____
_____
_____
_____
_____
_____
_____
_____

CLOSING SHIFT SIGNATURE	STARTING SHIFT SIGNATURE

SHIFT HANDOVER

DATE		DAY	
NAME		RANK / GRADE	
TIME IN		TIME OUT	
DEPARTMENT		SUPERVISOR	
HANDOVER TIME			

HANDOVER DETAILS	
EQUIPMENT	
CONCERNS	

HANDOVER TO		STAFF NO.	
DATE IN		DATE OUT	
TIME IN		TIME OUT	

ACTIONS TO COMPLETE

NO.	ACTION	COMPLETED DATE
1		
2		
3		
4		
5		

COMPLETED ACTIONS

NO.	ACTION	COMPLETED DATE
1		
2		
3		
4		
5		

NOTES

_____

_____

_____

_____

_____

_____

_____

CLOSING SHIFT SIGNATURE	STARTING SHIFT SIGNATURE

SHIFT HANDOVER

DATE		DAY	
NAME		RANK / GRADE	
TIME IN		TIME OUT	
DEPARTMENT		SUPERVISOR	
HANDOVER TIME			

HANDOVER DETAILS	
EQUIPMENT	
CONCERNS	

HANDOVER TO		STAFF NO.	
DATE IN		DATE OUT	
TIME IN		TIME OUT	

ACTIONS TO COMPLETE

NO.	ACTION	COMPLETED DATE
1		
2		
3		
4		
5		

COMPLETED ACTIONS

NO.	ACTION	COMPLETED DATE
1		
2		
3		
4		
5		

NOTES

_____
_____
_____
_____
_____
_____
_____
_____

CLOSING SHIFT SIGNATURE	STARTING SHIFT SIGNATURE

SHIFT HANDOVER

DATE		DAY	
NAME		RANK / GRADE	
TIME IN		TIME OUT	
DEPARTMENT		SUPERVISOR	
HANDOVER TIME			

HANDOVER DETAILS	
EQUIPMENT	
CONCERNS	

HANDOVER TO		STAFF NO.	
DATE IN		DATE OUT	
TIME IN		TIME OUT	

ACTIONS TO COMPLETE

NO.	ACTION	COMPLETED DATE
1		
2		
3		
4		
5		

COMPLETED ACTIONS

NO.	ACTION	COMPLETED DATE
1		
2		
3		
4		
5		

NOTES

_____

_____

_____

_____

_____

_____

_____

_____

CLOSING SHIFT SIGNATURE	STARTING SHIFT SIGNATURE

SHIFT HANDOVER

DATE		DAY	
NAME		RANK / GRADE	
TIME IN		TIME OUT	
DEPARTMENT		SUPERVISOR	
HANDOVER TIME			

HANDOVER DETAILS	
EQUIPMENT	
CONCERNS	

HANDOVER TO		STAFF NO.	
DATE IN		DATE OUT	
TIME IN		TIME OUT	

ACTIONS TO COMPLETE

NO.	ACTION	COMPLETED DATE
1		
2		
3		
4		
5		

COMPLETED ACTIONS

NO.	ACTION	COMPLETED DATE
1		
2		
3		
4		
5		

NOTES

_____
_____
_____
_____
_____
_____
_____
_____

CLOSING SHIFT SIGNATURE	STARTING SHIFT SIGNATURE

SHIFT HANDOVER

DATE		DAY	
NAME		RANK / GRADE	
TIME IN		TIME OUT	
DEPARTMENT		SUPERVISOR	
HANDOVER TIME			

HANDOVER DETAILS	
EQUIPMENT	
CONCERNS	

HANDOVER TO		STAFF NO.	
DATE IN		DATE OUT	
TIME IN		TIME OUT	

ACTIONS TO COMPLETE

NO.	ACTION	COMPLETED DATE
1		
2		
3		
4		
5		

COMPLETED ACTIONS

NO.	ACTION	COMPLETED DATE
1		
2		
3		
4		
5		

NOTES

_____
_____
_____
_____
_____
_____
_____
_____

CLOSING SHIFT SIGNATURE	STARTING SHIFT SIGNATURE

SHIFT HANDOVER

DATE		DAY	
NAME		RANK / GRADE	
TIME IN		TIME OUT	
DEPARTMENT		SUPERVISOR	
HANDOVER TIME			

HANDOVER DETAILS	
EQUIPMENT	
CONCERNS	

HANDOVER TO		STAFF NO.	
DATE IN		DATE OUT	
TIME IN		TIME OUT	

ACTIONS TO COMPLETE

NO.	ACTION	COMPLETED DATE
1		
2		
3		
4		
5		

COMPLETED ACTIONS

NO.	ACTION	COMPLETED DATE
1		
2		
3		
4		
5		

NOTES

_____
_____
_____
_____
_____
_____
_____
_____

CLOSING SHIFT SIGNATURE	STARTING SHIFT SIGNATURE

SHIFT HANDOVER

DATE		DAY	
NAME		RANK / GRADE	
TIME IN		TIME OUT	
DEPARTMENT		SUPERVISOR	
HANDOVER TIME			

HANDOVER DETAILS	
EQUIPMENT	
CONCERNS	

HANDOVER TO		STAFF NO.	
DATE IN		DATE OUT	
TIME IN		TIME OUT	

ACTIONS TO COMPLETE

NO.	ACTION	COMPLETED DATE
1		
2		
3		
4		
5		

COMPLETED ACTIONS

NO.	ACTION	COMPLETED DATE
1		
2		
3		
4		
5		

NOTES

_____
_____
_____
_____
_____
_____
_____

CLOSING SHIFT SIGNATURE	STARTING SHIFT SIGNATURE

SHIFT HANDOVER

DATE		DAY	
NAME		RANK / GRADE	
TIME IN		TIME OUT	
DEPARTMENT		SUPERVISOR	
HANDOVER TIME			

HANDOVER DETAILS	

EQUIPMENT	

CONCERNS	

HANDOVER TO		STAFF NO.	
DATE IN		DATE OUT	
TIME IN		TIME OUT	

ACTIONS TO COMPLETE

NO.	ACTION	COMPLETED DATE
1		
2		
3		
4		
5		

COMPLETED ACTIONS

NO.	ACTION	COMPLETED DATE
1		
2		
3		
4		
5		

NOTES

_____
_____
_____
_____
_____
_____
_____
_____

CLOSING SHIFT SIGNATURE	STARTING SHIFT SIGNATURE

SHIFT HANDOVER

DATE		DAY	
NAME		RANK / GRADE	
TIME IN		TIME OUT	
DEPARTMENT		SUPERVISOR	
HANDOVER TIME			

HANDOVER DETAILS	
EQUIPMENT	
CONCERNS	

HANDOVER TO		STAFF NO.	
DATE IN		DATE OUT	
TIME IN		TIME OUT	

ACTIONS TO COMPLETE   COMPLETED ACTIONS

NO.	ACTION	COMPLETED DATE	NO.	ACTION	COMPLETED DATE
1			1		
2			2		
3			3		
4			4		
5			5		

NOTES

_____
_____
_____
_____
_____
_____
_____

CLOSING SHIFT SIGNATURE	STARTING SHIFT SIGNATURE

SHIFT HANDOVER

DATE		DAY	
NAME		RANK / GRADE	
TIME IN		TIME OUT	
DEPARTMENT		SUPERVISOR	
HANDOVER TIME			

HANDOVER DETAILS	
EQUIPMENT	
CONCERNS	

HANDOVER TO		STAFF NO.	
DATE IN		DATE OUT	
TIME IN		TIME OUT	

ACTIONS TO COMPLETE

NO.	ACTION	COMPLETED DATE
1		
2		
3		
4		
5		

COMPLETED ACTIONS

NO.	ACTION	COMPLETED DATE
1		
2		
3		
4		
5		

NOTES

_____
_____
_____
_____
_____
_____
_____
_____

CLOSING SHIFT SIGNATURE	STARTING SHIFT SIGNATURE

SHIFT HANDOVER

DATE		DAY	
NAME		RANK / GRADE	
TIME IN		TIME OUT	
DEPARTMENT		SUPERVISOR	
HANDOVER TIME			

HANDOVER DETAILS	
EQUIPMENT	
CONCERNS	

HANDOVER TO		STAFF NO.	
DATE IN		DATE OUT	
TIME IN		TIME OUT	

ACTIONS TO COMPLETE

COMPLETED ACTIONS

NO.	ACTION	COMPLETED DATE
1		
2		
3		
4		
5		

NO.	ACTION	COMPLETED DATE
1		
2		
3		
4		
5		

NOTES

_____
_____
_____
_____
_____
_____
_____
_____

CLOSING SHIFT SIGNATURE	STARTING SHIFT SIGNATURE

SHIFT HANDOVER

DATE		DAY	
NAME		RANK / GRADE	
TIME IN		TIME OUT	
DEPARTMENT		SUPERVISOR	
HANDOVER TIME			

HANDOVER DETAILS	
EQUIPMENT	
CONCERNS	

HANDOVER TO		STAFF NO.	
DATE IN		DATE OUT	
TIME IN		TIME OUT	

ACTIONS TO COMPLETE

NO.	ACTION	COMPLETED DATE
1		
2		
3		
4		
5		

COMPLETED ACTIONS

NO.	ACTION	COMPLETED DATE
1		
2		
3		
4		
5		

NOTES

_____
_____
_____
_____
_____
_____
_____
_____

CLOSING SHIFT SIGNATURE	STARTING SHIFT SIGNATURE

SHIFT HANDOVER

DATE		DAY	
NAME		RANK / GRADE	
TIME IN		TIME OUT	
DEPARTMENT		SUPERVISOR	
HANDOVER TIME			

HANDOVER DETAILS	
EQUIPMENT	
CONCERNS	

HANDOVER TO		STAFF NO.	
DATE IN		DATE OUT	
TIME IN		TIME OUT	

ACTIONS TO COMPLETE

NO.	ACTION	COMPLETED DATE
1		
2		
3		
4		
5		

COMPLETED ACTIONS

NO.	ACTION	COMPLETED DATE
1		
2		
3		
4		
5		

NOTES

_____
_____
_____
_____
_____
_____
_____

CLOSING SHIFT SIGNATURE	STARTING SHIFT SIGNATURE

SHIFT HANDOVER

DATE		DAY	
NAME		RANK / GRADE	
TIME IN		TIME OUT	
DEPARTMENT		SUPERVISOR	
HANDOVER TIME			

HANDOVER DETAILS	
EQUIPMENT	
CONCERNS	

HANDOVER TO		STAFF NO.	
DATE IN		DATE OUT	
TIME IN		TIME OUT	

ACTIONS TO COMPLETE

NO.	ACTION	COMPLETED DATE
1		
2		
3		
4		
5		

COMPLETED ACTIONS

NO.	ACTION	COMPLETED DATE
1		
2		
3		
4		
5		

NOTES

_____

_____

_____

_____

_____

_____

_____

_____

CLOSING SHIFT SIGNATURE	STARTING SHIFT SIGNATURE

SHIFT HANDOVER

DATE		DAY	
NAME		RANK / GRADE	
TIME IN		TIME OUT	
DEPARTMENT		SUPERVISOR	
HANDOVER TIME			

HANDOVER DETAILS	
EQUIPMENT	
CONCERNS	

HANDOVER TO		STAFF NO.	
DATE IN		DATE OUT	
TIME IN		TIME OUT	

ACTIONS TO COMPLETE   COMPLETED ACTIONS

NO.	ACTION	COMPLETED DATE	NO.	ACTION	COMPLETED DATE
1			1		
2			2		
3			3		
4			4		
5			5		

NOTES

_____

_____

_____

_____

_____

_____

_____

_____

CLOSING SHIFT SIGNATURE	STARTING SHIFT SIGNATURE

SHIFT HANDOVER

DATE		DAY	
NAME		RANK / GRADE	
TIME IN		TIME OUT	
DEPARTMENT		SUPERVISOR	
HANDOVER TIME			

HANDOVER DETAILS	
EQUIPMENT	
CONCERNS	

HANDOVER TO		STAFF NO.	
DATE IN		DATE OUT	
TIME IN		TIME OUT	

ACTIONS TO COMPLETE / COMPLETED ACTIONS

NO.	ACTION	COMPLETED DATE	NO.	ACTION	COMPLETED DATE
1			1		
2			2		
3			3		
4			4		
5			5		

NOTES

_____

_____

_____

_____

_____

_____

_____

_____

_____

CLOSING SHIFT SIGNATURE	STARTING SHIFT SIGNATURE

SHIFT HANDOVER

DATE		DAY	
NAME		RANK / GRADE	
TIME IN		TIME OUT	
DEPARTMENT		SUPERVISOR	
HANDOVER TIME			

HANDOVER DETAILS	
EQUIPMENT	
CONCERNS	

HANDOVER TO		STAFF NO.	
DATE IN		DATE OUT	
TIME IN		TIME OUT	

ACTIONS TO COMPLETE

COMPLETED ACTIONS

NO.	ACTION	COMPLETED DATE	NO.	ACTION	COMPLETED DATE
1			1		
2			2		
3			3		
4			4		
5			5		

NOTES

_____
_____
_____
_____
_____
_____
_____
_____

CLOSING SHIFT SIGNATURE	STARTING SHIFT SIGNATURE

SHIFT HANDOVER

DATE		DAY	
NAME		RANK / GRADE	
TIME IN		TIME OUT	
DEPARTMENT		SUPERVISOR	
HANDOVER TIME			

HANDOVER DETAILS	
EQUIPMENT	
CONCERNS	

HANDOVER TO		STAFF NO.	
DATE IN		DATE OUT	
TIME IN		TIME OUT	

ACTIONS TO COMPLETE

NO.	ACTION	COMPLETED DATE
1		
2		
3		
4		
5		

COMPLETED ACTIONS

NO.	ACTION	COMPLETED DATE
1		
2		
3		
4		
5		

NOTES

_____

_____

_____

_____

_____

_____

_____

_____

_____

CLOSING SHIFT SIGNATURE	STARTING SHIFT SIGNATURE

SHIFT HANDOVER

DATE		DAY	
NAME		RANK / GRADE	
TIME IN		TIME OUT	
DEPARTMENT		SUPERVISOR	
HANDOVER TIME			

HANDOVER DETAILS	

EQUIPMENT	

CONCERNS	

HANDOVER TO		STAFF NO.	
DATE IN		DATE OUT	
TIME IN		TIME OUT	

ACTIONS TO COMPLETE

COMPLETED ACTIONS

NO.	ACTION	COMPLETED DATE	NO.	ACTION	COMPLETED DATE
1			1		
2			2		
3			3		
4			4		
5			5		

NOTES

_____
_____
_____
_____
_____
_____
_____
_____

CLOSING SHIFT SIGNATURE	STARTING SHIFT SIGNATURE

SHIFT HANDOVER

DATE		DAY	
NAME		RANK / GRADE	
TIME IN		TIME OUT	
DEPARTMENT		SUPERVISOR	
HANDOVER TIME			

HANDOVER DETAILS	
EQUIPMENT	
CONCERNS	

HANDOVER TO		STAFF NO.	
DATE IN		DATE OUT	
TIME IN		TIME OUT	

ACTIONS TO COMPLETE

NO.	ACTION	COMPLETED DATE
1		
2		
3		
4		
5		

COMPLETED ACTIONS

NO.	ACTION	COMPLETED DATE
1		
2		
3		
4		
5		

NOTES

_____

_____

_____

_____

_____

_____

_____

_____

CLOSING SHIFT SIGNATURE	STARTING SHIFT SIGNATURE

SHIFT HANDOVER

DATE		DAY	
NAME		RANK / GRADE	
TIME IN		TIME OUT	
DEPARTMENT		SUPERVISOR	
HANDOVER TIME			

HANDOVER DETAILS	
EQUIPMENT	
CONCERNS	

HANDOVER TO		STAFF NO.	
DATE IN		DATE OUT	
TIME IN		TIME OUT	

ACTIONS TO COMPLETE

NO.	ACTION	COMPLETED DATE
1		
2		
3		
4		
5		

COMPLETED ACTIONS

NO.	ACTION	COMPLETED DATE
1		
2		
3		
4		
5		

NOTES

_____
_____
_____
_____
_____
_____
_____
_____

CLOSING SHIFT SIGNATURE	STARTING SHIFT SIGNATURE

SHIFT HANDOVER

DATE		DAY	
NAME		RANK / GRADE	
TIME IN		TIME OUT	
DEPARTMENT		SUPERVISOR	
HANDOVER TIME			

HANDOVER DETAILS	
EQUIPMENT	
CONCERNS	

HANDOVER TO		STAFF NO.	
DATE IN		DATE OUT	
TIME IN		TIME OUT	

ACTIONS TO COMPLETE

NO.	ACTION	COMPLETED DATE
1		
2		
3		
4		
5		

COMPLETED ACTIONS

NO.	ACTION	COMPLETED DATE
1		
2		
3		
4		
5		

NOTES

_____
_____
_____
_____
_____
_____
_____
_____

CLOSING SHIFT SIGNATURE	STARTING SHIFT SIGNATURE

SHIFT HANDOVER

DATE		DAY	
NAME		RANK / GRADE	
TIME IN		TIME OUT	
DEPARTMENT		SUPERVISOR	
HANDOVER TIME			

HANDOVER DETAILS	
EQUIPMENT	
CONCERNS	

HANDOVER TO		STAFF NO.	
DATE IN		DATE OUT	
TIME IN		TIME OUT	

ACTIONS TO COMPLETE

COMPLETED ACTIONS

NO.	ACTION	COMPLETED DATE
1		
2		
3		
4		
5		

NO.	ACTION	COMPLETED DATE
1		
2		
3		
4		
5		

NOTES

_____

_____

_____

_____

_____

_____

_____

CLOSING SHIFT SIGNATURE	STARTING SHIFT SIGNATURE

SHIFT HANDOVER

DATE		DAY	
NAME		RANK / GRADE	
TIME IN		TIME OUT	
DEPARTMENT		SUPERVISOR	
HANDOVER TIME			

HANDOVER DETAILS	
EQUIPMENT	
CONCERNS	

HANDOVER TO		STAFF NO.	
DATE IN		DATE OUT	
TIME IN		TIME OUT	

ACTIONS TO COMPLETE   COMPLETED ACTIONS

NO.	ACTION	COMPLETED DATE	NO.	ACTION	COMPLETED DATE
1			1		
2			2		
3			3		
4			4		
5			5		

NOTES

_____
_____
_____
_____
_____
_____
_____
_____

CLOSING SHIFT SIGNATURE	STARTING SHIFT SIGNATURE

SHIFT HANDOVER

DATE		DAY	
NAME		RANK / GRADE	
TIME IN		TIME OUT	
DEPARTMENT		SUPERVISOR	
HANDOVER TIME			

HANDOVER DETAILS	
EQUIPMENT	
CONCERNS	

HANDOVER TO		STAFF NO.	
DATE IN		DATE OUT	
TIME IN		TIME OUT	

ACTIONS TO COMPLETE

NO.	ACTION	COMPLETED DATE
1		
2		
3		
4		
5		

COMPLETED ACTIONS

NO.	ACTION	COMPLETED DATE
1		
2		
3		
4		
5		

NOTES

_____

_____

_____

_____

_____

_____

_____

CLOSING SHIFT SIGNATURE	STARTING SHIFT SIGNATURE

SHIFT HANDOVER

DATE		DAY	
NAME		RANK / GRADE	
TIME IN		TIME OUT	
DEPARTMENT		SUPERVISOR	
HANDOVER TIME			

HANDOVER DETAILS	
EQUIPMENT	
CONCERNS	

HANDOVER TO		STAFF NO.	
DATE IN		DATE OUT	
TIME IN		TIME OUT	

ACTIONS TO COMPLETE

NO.	ACTION	COMPLETED DATE
1		
2		
3		
4		
5		

COMPLETED ACTIONS

NO.	ACTION	COMPLETED DATE
1		
2		
3		
4		
5		

NOTES

_____

_____

_____

_____

_____

_____

_____

_____

CLOSING SHIFT SIGNATURE	STARTING SHIFT SIGNATURE

SHIFT HANDOVER

DATE		DAY	
NAME		RANK / GRADE	
TIME IN		TIME OUT	
DEPARTMENT		SUPERVISOR	
HANDOVER TIME			

HANDOVER DETAILS	
EQUIPMENT	
CONCERNS	

HANDOVER TO		STAFF NO.	
DATE IN		DATE OUT	
TIME IN		TIME OUT	

ACTIONS TO COMPLETE   COMPLETED ACTIONS

NO.	ACTION	COMPLETED DATE	NO.	ACTION	COMPLETED DATE
1			1		
2			2		
3			3		
4			4		
5			5		

NOTES

_____
_____
_____
_____
_____
_____
_____
_____

CLOSING SHIFT SIGNATURE	STARTING SHIFT SIGNATURE

SHIFT HANDOVER

DATE		DAY	
NAME		RANK / GRADE	
TIME IN		TIME OUT	
DEPARTMENT		SUPERVISOR	
HANDOVER TIME			

HANDOVER DETAILS	
EQUIPMENT	
CONCERNS	

HANDOVER TO		STAFF NO.	
DATE IN		DATE OUT	
TIME IN		TIME OUT	

ACTIONS TO COMPLETE

NO.	ACTION	COMPLETED DATE
1		
2		
3		
4		
5		

COMPLETED ACTIONS

NO.	ACTION	COMPLETED DATE
1		
2		
3		
4		
5		

NOTES

_____

_____

_____

_____

_____

_____

_____

_____

_____

CLOSING SHIFT SIGNATURE	STARTING SHIFT SIGNATURE

SHIFT HANDOVER

DATE		DAY	
NAME		RANK / GRADE	
TIME IN		TIME OUT	
DEPARTMENT		SUPERVISOR	
HANDOVER TIME			

HANDOVER DETAILS	
EQUIPMENT	
CONCERNS	

HANDOVER TO		STAFF NO.	
DATE IN		DATE OUT	
TIME IN		TIME OUT	

ACTIONS TO COMPLETE

NO.	ACTION	COMPLETED DATE
1		
2		
3		
4		
5		

COMPLETED ACTIONS

NO.	ACTION	COMPLETED DATE
1		
2		
3		
4		
5		

NOTES

_____
_____
_____
_____
_____
_____
_____
_____

CLOSING SHIFT SIGNATURE	STARTING SHIFT SIGNATURE

SHIFT HANDOVER

DATE		DAY	
NAME		RANK / GRADE	
TIME IN		TIME OUT	
DEPARTMENT		SUPERVISOR	
HANDOVER TIME			

HANDOVER DETAILS	
EQUIPMENT	
CONCERNS	

HANDOVER TO		STAFF NO.	
DATE IN		DATE OUT	
TIME IN		TIME OUT	

ACTIONS TO COMPLETE

NO.	ACTION	COMPLETED DATE
1		
2		
3		
4		
5		

COMPLETED ACTIONS

NO.	ACTION	COMPLETED DATE
1		
2		
3		
4		
5		

NOTES

_____
_____
_____
_____
_____
_____
_____
_____

CLOSING SHIFT SIGNATURE	STARTING SHIFT SIGNATURE

SHIFT HANDOVER

DATE		DAY	
NAME		RANK / GRADE	
TIME IN		TIME OUT	
DEPARTMENT		SUPERVISOR	
HANDOVER TIME			

HANDOVER DETAILS	
EQUIPMENT	
CONCERNS	

HANDOVER TO		STAFF NO.	
DATE IN		DATE OUT	
TIME IN		TIME OUT	

ACTIONS TO COMPLETE

NO.	ACTION	COMPLETED DATE
1		
2		
3		
4		
5		

COMPLETED ACTIONS

NO.	ACTION	COMPLETED DATE
1		
2		
3		
4		
5		

NOTES

_____

_____

_____

_____

_____

_____

_____

_____

CLOSING SHIFT SIGNATURE	**STARTING SHIFT SIGNATURE**

SHIFT HANDOVER

DATE		DAY	
NAME		RANK / GRADE	
TIME IN		TIME OUT	
DEPARTMENT		SUPERVISOR	
HANDOVER TIME			

HANDOVER DETAILS	

EQUIPMENT	

CONCERNS	

HANDOVER TO		STAFF NO.	
DATE IN		DATE OUT	
TIME IN		TIME OUT	

ACTIONS TO COMPLETE

NO.	ACTION	COMPLETED DATE
1		
2		
3		
4		
5		

COMPLETED ACTIONS

NO.	ACTION	COMPLETED DATE
1		
2		
3		
4		
5		

NOTES

_____
_____
_____
_____
_____
_____
_____
_____
_____

CLOSING SHIFT SIGNATURE	STARTING SHIFT SIGNATURE

SHIFT HANDOVER

DATE		DAY	
NAME		RANK / GRADE	
TIME IN		TIME OUT	
DEPARTMENT		SUPERVISOR	
HANDOVER TIME			

HANDOVER DETAILS	
EQUIPMENT	
CONCERNS	

HANDOVER TO		STAFF NO.	
DATE IN		DATE OUT	
TIME IN		TIME OUT	

ACTIONS TO COMPLETE

NO.	ACTION	COMPLETED DATE
1		
2		
3		
4		
5		

COMPLETED ACTIONS

NO.	ACTION	COMPLETED DATE
1		
2		
3		
4		
5		

NOTES

_____
_____
_____
_____
_____
_____
_____
_____

CLOSING SHIFT SIGNATURE	STARTING SHIFT SIGNATURE

SHIFT HANDOVER

DATE		DAY	
NAME		RANK / GRADE	
TIME IN		TIME OUT	
DEPARTMENT		SUPERVISOR	
HANDOVER TIME			

HANDOVER DETAILS	
EQUIPMENT	
CONCERNS	

HANDOVER TO		STAFF NO.	
DATE IN		DATE OUT	
TIME IN		TIME OUT	

ACTIONS TO COMPLETE

NO.	ACTION	COMPLETED DATE
1		
2		
3		
4		
5		

COMPLETED ACTIONS

NO.	ACTION	COMPLETED DATE
1		
2		
3		
4		
5		

NOTES

_____
_____
_____
_____
_____
_____
_____
_____

CLOSING SHIFT SIGNATURE	STARTING SHIFT SIGNATURE

SHIFT HANDOVER

DATE		DAY	
NAME		RANK / GRADE	
TIME IN		TIME OUT	
DEPARTMENT		SUPERVISOR	
HANDOVER TIME			

HANDOVER DETAILS	
EQUIPMENT	
CONCERNS	

HANDOVER TO		STAFF NO.	
DATE IN		DATE OUT	
TIME IN		TIME OUT	

ACTIONS TO COMPLETE

NO.	ACTION	COMPLETED DATE
1		
2		
3		
4		
5		

COMPLETED ACTIONS

NO.	ACTION	COMPLETED DATE
1		
2		
3		
4		
5		

NOTES

_____
_____
_____
_____
_____
_____
_____
_____
_____

CLOSING SHIFT SIGNATURE	STARTING SHIFT SIGNATURE

SHIFT HANDOVER

DATE		DAY	
NAME		RANK / GRADE	
TIME IN		TIME OUT	
DEPARTMENT		SUPERVISOR	
HANDOVER TIME			

HANDOVER DETAILS	

EQUIPMENT	

CONCERNS	

HANDOVER TO		STAFF NO.	
DATE IN		DATE OUT	
TIME IN		TIME OUT	

ACTIONS TO COMPLETE

NO.	ACTION	COMPLETED DATE
1		
2		
3		
4		
5		

COMPLETED ACTIONS

NO.	ACTION	COMPLETED DATE
1		
2		
3		
4		
5		

NOTES

_____
_____
_____
_____
_____
_____
_____
_____

CLOSING SHIFT SIGNATURE	STARTING SHIFT SIGNATURE

SHIFT HANDOVER

DATE		DAY	
NAME		RANK / GRADE	
TIME IN		TIME OUT	
DEPARTMENT		SUPERVISOR	
HANDOVER TIME			

HANDOVER DETAILS	
EQUIPMENT	
CONCERNS	

HANDOVER TO		STAFF NO.	
DATE IN		DATE OUT	
TIME IN		TIME OUT	

ACTIONS TO COMPLETE

NO.	ACTION	COMPLETED DATE
1		
2		
3		
4		
5		

COMPLETED ACTIONS

NO.	ACTION	COMPLETED DATE
1		
2		
3		
4		
5		

NOTES

_____
_____
_____
_____
_____
_____
_____
_____

CLOSING SHIFT SIGNATURE	STARTING SHIFT SIGNATURE

SHIFT HANDOVER

DATE		DAY	
NAME		RANK / GRADE	
TIME IN		TIME OUT	
DEPARTMENT		SUPERVISOR	
HANDOVER TIME			

HANDOVER DETAILS	

EQUIPMENT	

CONCERNS	

HANDOVER TO		STAFF NO.	
DATE IN		DATE OUT	
TIME IN		TIME OUT	

ACTIONS TO COMPLETE   COMPLETED ACTIONS

NO.	ACTION	COMPLETED DATE	NO.	ACTION	COMPLETED DATE
1			1		
2			2		
3			3		
4			4		
5			5		

NOTES

_____
_____
_____
_____
_____
_____
_____

CLOSING SHIFT SIGNATURE	STARTING SHIFT SIGNATURE

SHIFT HANDOVER

DATE		DAY	
NAME		RANK / GRADE	
TIME IN		TIME OUT	
DEPARTMENT		SUPERVISOR	
HANDOVER TIME			

HANDOVER DETAILS	
EQUIPMENT	
CONCERNS	

HANDOVER TO		STAFF NO.	
DATE IN		DATE OUT	
TIME IN		TIME OUT	

ACTIONS TO COMPLETE

NO.	ACTION	COMPLETED DATE
1		
2		
3		
4		
5		

COMPLETED ACTIONS

NO.	ACTION	COMPLETED DATE
1		
2		
3		
4		
5		

NOTES

_____
_____
_____
_____
_____
_____
_____
_____

CLOSING SHIFT SIGNATURE	STARTING SHIFT SIGNATURE

SHIFT HANDOVER

DATE		DAY	
NAME		RANK / GRADE	
TIME IN		TIME OUT	
DEPARTMENT		SUPERVISOR	
HANDOVER TIME			

HANDOVER DETAILS	

EQUIPMENT	

CONCERNS	

HANDOVER TO		STAFF NO.	
DATE IN		DATE OUT	
TIME IN		TIME OUT	

ACTIONS TO COMPLETE

NO.	ACTION	COMPLETED DATE
1		
2		
3		
4		
5		

COMPLETED ACTIONS

NO.	ACTION	COMPLETED DATE
1		
2		
3		
4		
5		

NOTES

_____
_____
_____
_____
_____
_____
_____
_____

CLOSING SHIFT SIGNATURE	STARTING SHIFT SIGNATURE

SHIFT HANDOVER

DATE		DAY	
NAME		RANK / GRADE	
TIME IN		TIME OUT	
DEPARTMENT		SUPERVISOR	
HANDOVER TIME			

HANDOVER DETAILS	

EQUIPMENT	

CONCERNS	

HANDOVER TO		STAFF NO.	
DATE IN		DATE OUT	
TIME IN		TIME OUT	

ACTIONS TO COMPLETE

NO.	ACTION	COMPLETED DATE
1		
2		
3		
4		
5		

COMPLETED ACTIONS

NO.	ACTION	COMPLETED DATE
1		
2		
3		
4		
5		

NOTES

_____

_____

_____

_____

_____

_____

_____

_____

CLOSING SHIFT SIGNATURE	STARTING SHIFT SIGNATURE

SHIFT HANDOVER

DATE		DAY	
NAME		RANK / GRADE	
TIME IN		TIME OUT	
DEPARTMENT		SUPERVISOR	
HANDOVER TIME			

HANDOVER DETAILS	
EQUIPMENT	
CONCERNS	

HANDOVER TO		STAFF NO.	
DATE IN		DATE OUT	
TIME IN		TIME OUT	

ACTIONS TO COMPLETE

NO.	ACTION	COMPLETED DATE
1		
2		
3		
4		
5		

COMPLETED ACTIONS

NO.	ACTION	COMPLETED DATE
1		
2		
3		
4		
5		

NOTES

_____
_____
_____
_____
_____
_____
_____
_____

CLOSING SHIFT SIGNATURE	STARTING SHIFT SIGNATURE

SHIFT HANDOVER

DATE		DAY	
NAME		RANK / GRADE	
TIME IN		TIME OUT	
DEPARTMENT		SUPERVISOR	
HANDOVER TIME			

HANDOVER DETAILS	
EQUIPMENT	
CONCERNS	

HANDOVER TO		STAFF NO.	
DATE IN		DATE OUT	
TIME IN		TIME OUT	

ACTIONS TO COMPLETE

COMPLETED ACTIONS

NO.	ACTION	COMPLETED DATE	NO.	ACTION	COMPLETED DATE
1			1		
2			2		
3			3		
4			4		
5			5		

NOTES

_____

_____

_____

_____

_____

_____

_____

_____

CLOSING SHIFT SIGNATURE	STARTING SHIFT SIGNATURE

SHIFT HANDOVER

DATE		DAY	
NAME		RANK / GRADE	
TIME IN		TIME OUT	
DEPARTMENT		SUPERVISOR	
HANDOVER TIME			

HANDOVER DETAILS	
EQUIPMENT	
CONCERNS	

HANDOVER TO		STAFF NO.	
DATE IN		DATE OUT	
TIME IN		TIME OUT	

ACTIONS TO COMPLETE

COMPLETED ACTIONS

NO.	ACTION	COMPLETED DATE
1		
2		
3		
4		
5		

NO.	ACTION	COMPLETED DATE
1		
2		
3		
4		
5		

NOTES

_____
_____
_____
_____
_____
_____
_____
_____

CLOSING SHIFT SIGNATURE	STARTING SHIFT SIGNATURE

SHIFT HANDOVER

DATE		DAY	
NAME		RANK / GRADE	
TIME IN		TIME OUT	
DEPARTMENT		SUPERVISOR	
HANDOVER TIME			

HANDOVER DETAILS	
EQUIPMENT	
CONCERNS	

HANDOVER TO		STAFF NO.	
DATE IN		DATE OUT	
TIME IN		TIME OUT	

ACTIONS TO COMPLETE

NO.	ACTION	COMPLETED DATE
1		
2		
3		
4		
5		

COMPLETED ACTIONS

NO.	ACTION	COMPLETED DATE
1		
2		
3		
4		
5		

NOTES

_____
_____
_____
_____
_____
_____
_____
_____

CLOSING SHIFT SIGNATURE	STARTING SHIFT SIGNATURE

SHIFT HANDOVER

DATE		DAY	
NAME		RANK / GRADE	
TIME IN		TIME OUT	
DEPARTMENT		SUPERVISOR	
HANDOVER TIME			

HANDOVER DETAILS	

EQUIPMENT	

CONCERNS	

HANDOVER TO		STAFF NO.	
DATE IN		DATE OUT	
TIME IN		TIME OUT	

ACTIONS TO COMPLETE

NO.	ACTION	COMPLETED DATE
1		
2		
3		
4		
5		

COMPLETED ACTIONS

NO.	ACTION	COMPLETED DATE
1		
2		
3		
4		
5		

NOTES

_____
_____
_____
_____
_____
_____
_____
_____

CLOSING SHIFT SIGNATURE	STARTING SHIFT SIGNATURE

SHIFT HANDOVER

DATE		DAY	
NAME		RANK / GRADE	
TIME IN		TIME OUT	
DEPARTMENT		SUPERVISOR	
HANDOVER TIME			

HANDOVER DETAILS	
EQUIPMENT	
CONCERNS	

HANDOVER TO		STAFF NO.	
DATE IN		DATE OUT	
TIME IN		TIME OUT	

ACTIONS TO COMPLETE

NO.	ACTION	COMPLETED DATE
1		
2		
3		
4		
5		

COMPLETED ACTIONS

NO.	ACTION	COMPLETED DATE
1		
2		
3		
4		
5		

NOTES

_____
_____
_____
_____
_____
_____
_____
_____

CLOSING SHIFT SIGNATURE	STARTING SHIFT SIGNATURE

SHIFT HANDOVER

DATE		DAY	
NAME		RANK / GRADE	
TIME IN		TIME OUT	
DEPARTMENT		SUPERVISOR	
HANDOVER TIME			

HANDOVER DETAILS	
EQUIPMENT	
CONCERNS	

HANDOVER TO		STAFF NO.	
DATE IN		DATE OUT	
TIME IN		TIME OUT	

ACTIONS TO COMPLETE

NO.	ACTION	COMPLETED DATE
1		
2		
3		
4		
5		

COMPLETED ACTIONS

NO.	ACTION	COMPLETED DATE
1		
2		
3		
4		
5		

NOTES

_____

_____

_____

_____

_____

_____

_____

CLOSING SHIFT SIGNATURE	STARTING SHIFT SIGNATURE

SHIFT HANDOVER

DATE		DAY	
NAME		RANK / GRADE	
TIME IN		TIME OUT	
DEPARTMENT		SUPERVISOR	
HANDOVER TIME			

HANDOVER DETAILS	
EQUIPMENT	
CONCERNS	

HANDOVER TO		STAFF NO.	
DATE IN		DATE OUT	
TIME IN		TIME OUT	

ACTIONS TO COMPLETE

NO.	ACTION	COMPLETED DATE
1		
2		
3		
4		
5		

COMPLETED ACTIONS

NO.	ACTION	COMPLETED DATE
1		
2		
3		
4		
5		

NOTES

_____
_____
_____
_____
_____
_____
_____

CLOSING SHIFT SIGNATURE	STARTING SHIFT SIGNATURE

SHIFT HANDOVER

DATE		DAY	
NAME		RANK / GRADE	
TIME IN		TIME OUT	
DEPARTMENT		SUPERVISOR	
HANDOVER TIME			

HANDOVER DETAILS	
EQUIPMENT	
CONCERNS	

HANDOVER TO		STAFF NO.	
DATE IN		DATE OUT	
TIME IN		TIME OUT	

ACTIONS TO COMPLETE

NO.	ACTION	COMPLETED DATE
1		
2		
3		
4		
5		

COMPLETED ACTIONS

NO.	ACTION	COMPLETED DATE
1		
2		
3		
4		
5		

NOTES

_____
_____
_____
_____
_____
_____
_____
_____

CLOSING SHIFT SIGNATURE	STARTING SHIFT SIGNATURE

SHIFT HANDOVER

DATE		DAY	
NAME		RANK / GRADE	
TIME IN		TIME OUT	
DEPARTMENT		SUPERVISOR	
HANDOVER TIME			

HANDOVER DETAILS	
EQUIPMENT	
CONCERNS	

HANDOVER TO		STAFF NO.	
DATE IN		DATE OUT	
TIME IN		TIME OUT	

ACTIONS TO COMPLETE

NO.	ACTION	COMPLETED DATE
1		
2		
3		
4		
5		

COMPLETED ACTIONS

NO.	ACTION	COMPLETED DATE
1		
2		
3		
4		
5		

NOTES

_____
_____
_____
_____
_____
_____
_____
_____

CLOSING SHIFT SIGNATURE	STARTING SHIFT SIGNATURE

SHIFT HANDOVER

DATE		DAY	
NAME		RANK / GRADE	
TIME IN		TIME OUT	
DEPARTMENT		SUPERVISOR	
HANDOVER TIME			

HANDOVER DETAILS	
EQUIPMENT	
CONCERNS	

HANDOVER TO		STAFF NO.	
DATE IN		DATE OUT	
TIME IN		TIME OUT	

ACTIONS TO COMPLETE

COMPLETED ACTIONS

NO.	ACTION	COMPLETED DATE
1		
2		
3		
4		
5		

NO.	ACTION	COMPLETED DATE
1		
2		
3		
4		
5		

NOTES

_____

_____

_____

_____

_____

_____

_____

_____

CLOSING SHIFT SIGNATURE	STARTING SHIFT SIGNATURE

SHIFT HANDOVER

DATE		DAY	
NAME		RANK / GRADE	
TIME IN		TIME OUT	
DEPARTMENT		SUPERVISOR	
HANDOVER TIME			

HANDOVER DETAILS	
EQUIPMENT	
CONCERNS	

HANDOVER TO		STAFF NO.	
DATE IN		DATE OUT	
TIME IN		TIME OUT	

ACTIONS TO COMPLETE

COMPLETED ACTIONS

NO.	ACTION	COMPLETED DATE
1		
2		
3		
4		
5		

NO.	ACTION	COMPLETED DATE
1		
2		
3		
4		
5		

NOTES

_____

_____

_____

_____

_____

_____

_____

_____

CLOSING SHIFT SIGNATURE	STARTING SHIFT SIGNATURE

SHIFT HANDOVER

DATE		DAY	
NAME		RANK / GRADE	
TIME IN		TIME OUT	
DEPARTMENT		SUPERVISOR	
HANDOVER TIME			

HANDOVER DETAILS	
EQUIPMENT	
CONCERNS	

HANDOVER TO		STAFF NO.	
DATE IN		DATE OUT	
TIME IN		TIME OUT	

ACTIONS TO COMPLETE

NO.	ACTION	COMPLETED DATE
1		
2		
3		
4		
5		

COMPLETED ACTIONS

NO.	ACTION	COMPLETED DATE
1		
2		
3		
4		
5		

NOTES

_____

_____

_____

_____

_____

_____

_____

CLOSING SHIFT SIGNATURE	STARTING SHIFT SIGNATURE

SHIFT HANDOVER

DATE		DAY	
NAME		RANK / GRADE	
TIME IN		TIME OUT	
DEPARTMENT		SUPERVISOR	
HANDOVER TIME			

HANDOVER DETAILS	
EQUIPMENT	
CONCERNS	

HANDOVER TO		STAFF NO.	
DATE IN		DATE OUT	
TIME IN		TIME OUT	

ACTIONS TO COMPLETE   COMPLETED ACTIONS

NO.	ACTION	COMPLETED DATE	NO.	ACTION	COMPLETED DATE
1			1		
2			2		
3			3		
4			4		
5			5		

NOTES

_____
_____
_____
_____
_____
_____
_____
_____

CLOSING SHIFT SIGNATURE	STARTING SHIFT SIGNATURE

SHIFT HANDOVER

DATE		DAY	
NAME		RANK / GRADE	
TIME IN		TIME OUT	
DEPARTMENT		SUPERVISOR	
HANDOVER TIME			

HANDOVER DETAILS	
EQUIPMENT	
CONCERNS	

HANDOVER TO		STAFF NO.	
DATE IN		DATE OUT	
TIME IN		TIME OUT	

ACTIONS TO COMPLETE

NO.	ACTION	COMPLETED DATE
1		
2		
3		
4		
5		

COMPLETED ACTIONS

NO.	ACTION	COMPLETED DATE
1		
2		
3		
4		
5		

NOTES

_____
_____
_____
_____
_____
_____
_____
_____

CLOSING SHIFT SIGNATURE	STARTING SHIFT SIGNATURE

SHIFT HANDOVER

DATE		DAY	
NAME		RANK / GRADE	
TIME IN		TIME OUT	
DEPARTMENT		SUPERVISOR	
HANDOVER TIME			

HANDOVER DETAILS	
EQUIPMENT	
CONCERNS	

HANDOVER TO		STAFF NO.	
DATE IN		DATE OUT	
TIME IN		TIME OUT	

ACTIONS TO COMPLETE

COMPLETED ACTIONS

NO.	ACTION	COMPLETED DATE
1		
2		
3		
4		
5		

NO.	ACTION	COMPLETED DATE
1		
2		
3		
4		
5		

NOTES

CLOSING SHIFT SIGNATURE	STARTING SHIFT SIGNATURE

SHIFT HANDOVER

DATE		DAY	
NAME		RANK / GRADE	
TIME IN		TIME OUT	
DEPARTMENT		SUPERVISOR	
HANDOVER TIME			

HANDOVER DETAILS	
EQUIPMENT	
CONCERNS	

HANDOVER TO		STAFF NO.	
DATE IN		DATE OUT	
TIME IN		TIME OUT	

ACTIONS TO COMPLETE

NO.	ACTION	COMPLETED DATE
1		
2		
3		
4		
5		

COMPLETED ACTIONS

NO.	ACTION	COMPLETED DATE
1		
2		
3		
4		
5		

NOTES

_____
_____
_____
_____
_____
_____
_____
_____
_____

CLOSING SHIFT SIGNATURE	STARTING SHIFT SIGNATURE

SHIFT HANDOVER

DATE		DAY	
NAME		RANK / GRADE	
TIME IN		TIME OUT	
DEPARTMENT		SUPERVISOR	
HANDOVER TIME			

HANDOVER DETAILS	
EQUIPMENT	
CONCERNS	

HANDOVER TO		STAFF NO.	
DATE IN		DATE OUT	
TIME IN		TIME OUT	

ACTIONS TO COMPLETE

NO.	ACTION	COMPLETED DATE
1		
2		
3		
4		
5		

COMPLETED ACTIONS

NO.	ACTION	COMPLETED DATE
1		
2		
3		
4		
5		

NOTES

CLOSING SHIFT SIGNATURE	STARTING SHIFT SIGNATURE

SHIFT HANDOVER

DATE		DAY	
NAME		RANK / GRADE	
TIME IN		TIME OUT	
DEPARTMENT		SUPERVISOR	
HANDOVER TIME			

HANDOVER DETAILS	

EQUIPMENT	

CONCERNS	

HANDOVER TO		STAFF NO.	
DATE IN		DATE OUT	
TIME IN		TIME OUT	

ACTIONS TO COMPLETE   COMPLETED ACTIONS

NO.	ACTION	COMPLETED DATE	NO.	ACTION	COMPLETED DATE
1			1		
2			2		
3			3		
4			4		
5			5		

NOTES

_____
_____
_____
_____
_____
_____
_____
_____

CLOSING SHIFT SIGNATURE	STARTING SHIFT SIGNATURE

SHIFT HANDOVER

DATE		DAY	
NAME		RANK / GRADE	
TIME IN		TIME OUT	
DEPARTMENT		SUPERVISOR	
HANDOVER TIME			

HANDOVER DETAILS	
EQUIPMENT	
CONCERNS	

HANDOVER TO		STAFF NO.	
DATE IN		DATE OUT	
TIME IN		TIME OUT	

ACTIONS TO COMPLETE

COMPLETED ACTIONS

NO.	ACTION	COMPLETED DATE
1		
2		
3		
4		
5		

NO.	ACTION	COMPLETED DATE
1		
2		
3		
4		
5		

NOTES

_____
_____
_____
_____
_____
_____
_____
_____

CLOSING SHIFT SIGNATURE	STARTING SHIFT SIGNATURE

SHIFT HANDOVER

DATE		DAY	
NAME		RANK / GRADE	
TIME IN		TIME OUT	
DEPARTMENT		SUPERVISOR	
HANDOVER TIME			

HANDOVER DETAILS	
EQUIPMENT	
CONCERNS	

HANDOVER TO		STAFF NO.	
DATE IN		DATE OUT	
TIME IN		TIME OUT	

ACTIONS TO COMPLETE

NO.	ACTION	COMPLETED DATE
1		
2		
3		
4		
5		

COMPLETED ACTIONS

NO.	ACTION	COMPLETED DATE
1		
2		
3		
4		
5		

NOTES

_____
_____
_____
_____
_____
_____
_____
_____

CLOSING SHIFT SIGNATURE	STARTING SHIFT SIGNATURE

SHIFT HANDOVER

DATE		DAY	
NAME		RANK / GRADE	
TIME IN		TIME OUT	
DEPARTMENT		SUPERVISOR	
HANDOVER TIME			

HANDOVER DETAILS	
EQUIPMENT	
CONCERNS	

HANDOVER TO		STAFF NO.	
DATE IN		DATE OUT	
TIME IN		TIME OUT	

ACTIONS TO COMPLETE

COMPLETED ACTIONS

NO.	ACTION	COMPLETED DATE
1		
2		
3		
4		
5		

NO.	ACTION	COMPLETED DATE
1		
2		
3		
4		
5		

NOTES

_____

_____

_____

_____

_____

_____

_____

_____

CLOSING SHIFT SIGNATURE	STARTING SHIFT SIGNATURE

SHIFT HANDOVER

DATE		DAY	
NAME		RANK / GRADE	
TIME IN		TIME OUT	
DEPARTMENT		SUPERVISOR	
HANDOVER TIME			

HANDOVER DETAILS	
EQUIPMENT	
CONCERNS	

HANDOVER TO		STAFF NO.	
DATE IN		DATE OUT	
TIME IN		TIME OUT	

ACTIONS TO COMPLETE

NO.	ACTION	COMPLETED DATE
1		
2		
3		
4		
5		

COMPLETED ACTIONS

NO.	ACTION	COMPLETED DATE
1		
2		
3		
4		
5		

NOTES

_____
_____
_____
_____
_____
_____
_____
_____

CLOSING SHIFT SIGNATURE	STARTING SHIFT SIGNATURE

SHIFT HANDOVER

DATE		DAY	
NAME		RANK / GRADE	
TIME IN		TIME OUT	
DEPARTMENT		SUPERVISOR	
HANDOVER TIME			

HANDOVER DETAILS	
EQUIPMENT	
CONCERNS	

HANDOVER TO		STAFF NO.	
DATE IN		DATE OUT	
TIME IN		TIME OUT	

ACTIONS TO COMPLETE

NO.	ACTION	COMPLETED DATE
1		
2		
3		
4		
5		

COMPLETED ACTIONS

NO.	ACTION	COMPLETED DATE
1		
2		
3		
4		
5		

NOTES

_____
_____
_____
_____
_____
_____
_____
_____

CLOSING SHIFT SIGNATURE	STARTING SHIFT SIGNATURE

SHIFT HANDOVER

DATE		DAY	
NAME		RANK / GRADE	
TIME IN		TIME OUT	
DEPARTMENT		SUPERVISOR	
HANDOVER TIME			

HANDOVER DETAILS	
EQUIPMENT	
CONCERNS	

HANDOVER TO		STAFF NO.	
DATE IN		DATE OUT	
TIME IN		TIME OUT	

ACTIONS TO COMPLETE

COMPLETED ACTIONS

NO.	ACTION	COMPLETED DATE
1		
2		
3		
4		
5		

NO.	ACTION	COMPLETED DATE
1		
2		
3		
4		
5		

NOTES

_____
_____
_____
_____
_____
_____
_____
_____

CLOSING SHIFT SIGNATURE	STARTING SHIFT SIGNATURE

Made in the USA
Las Vegas, NV
28 December 2024

15508336R00070